Chasing Bruce

Confessions of a Springsteen Fan

by
Lori Krein

With contributions from:
Jeffrey Carhart
Phil Beard
Lenny B.
Bob Fuller
Jimmy Baron
Scott Elbaum

2025 Mariposa Publishing
Copyright @ 2025 by Lori Krein

LoriKrein.com
LoriKrein@gmail.com

All rights reserved
4/25/2025

Paperback
ISBN 978-1-7374599-9-6

Book cover design by Lori Krein

This book would not exist without the support of my writing community and Project Write Now, a nonprofit organization transforming individuals, organizations, and communities through writing.

To learn more, visit http://www.projectwritenow.org

ALSO BY LORI KREIN
Available on Amazon

Poetry and Memoir

Reason to Believe:
A Collection of Poetry

Hilda's Story: Surviving the Holocaust
My Grandmother's Story

Meditation in Manhattan:
Finding Calm in a Chaotic World

Children's Books

Clean Bee
Goodnight Bee
Green Bee
Learn Chess

Visit **LoriKrein.com** to learn more
@LoriKreinStudios (instagram)

Visit **Chasing Bruce** on Facebook to share YOUR stories!

This book is dedicated to:

Patty
My life-long Springsteen buddy and friend,
who understands the true meaning of fences.

Jason and Kevin
Who taught me that it's ok to go to a Bruce concert
instead of staying home to make them dinner.

The other Bruce in my life
Who, although he didn't always show it,
enjoyed the concerts as much as I did.

Teddy
A kindred spirit in music, dance and all things creative.

"Music is the great uniter" - Sarah Dessen

"Music gives a soul to the universe, wings to the mind, flight to the imagination, and life to everything." -Plato

"The best music is…there to provide you something to face the world with." — Bruce Springsteen

Table of Contents

Forward	2
Part 1: Lori's Stories	7
1979: The Fast Lane, Asbury Park, NJ	7
1981: Big Man's West, Red Bank, NJ	10
1995: Ghost of Tom Joad Tour	17
2007: Magic Tour, Oakland Arena	20
2007: Magic Tour, Part 2, Washington DC	23
2012: The Wrecking Ball Tour, Anaheim, CA	26
2016: The River Tour #2	30
2023: Portland, Oregon	31
2024: Sea Hear Now Festival, Asbury Park, NJ	34
My concert history	36
Part 2: Stories from other fans	43
A lifetime fan meets Bruce: Jeffrey Carhart – Toronto	44
A Journey from Liverpool to Freehold - Phil Beard	52
Lenny from NJ	60
Bob Fuller, Staten Island NY	61
Jimmy Baron, Atlanta, GA	62
Tribute to Brady	64
Afterward	66

Forward

In October 1975, when Bruce Springsteen hit the covers of both *TIME* **and** *Newsweek* magazines, I was 14 years old, and living in Freehold Township, NJ, a suburban bedroom community about 40 miles south of New York City. Freehold Township was adjacent to Freehold Boro, where Bruce grew up. The Boro was the more historic part of town with tree-lined streets, quaint Victorian homes, restaurants, shops, and City Hall, where Bruce's mom worked for many years, just a few blocks from where my mom worked for New Jersey Bell. I sometimes wonder if they ever crossed paths back then.

I have fond memories of the Boro from childhood; going to the bank and post office with my mom, the occasional family dinner at Federici's, and Jersey Freeze for a chocolate dip top.

Asbury Park was also part of my childhood. While Bruce was working on his first two albums in the early 70's, and playing at the local clubs, I was just a little girl, visiting Asbury with my family to go on the rides and eat boardwalk fries. Now, 50 years later, I live just a few blocks from that very same boardwalk. Even though the landscape has changed, I still feel a connection. The old casino and carousel building, in need of repair, stands tall and proud, filled with memories of days gone by.

In my 20's, I experienced another side of Asbury; the music. The Stone Pony and the Fast Lane were our go-to bars for great music, where me and my friends would dance the night away until 3am. Aside from live music and dancing, my other hobby was chasing boys. In my late teens, I started chasing one particular boy.

The chase continues to this day.

Born to Run

In the spring of 1975, Springsteen was on tour, performing songs from his first two albums, *Greetings From Asbury Park* and *The Wild, Innocent and the E Street Shuffle*, while working on the production of *Born to Run*. His goal, at the age of 24, was to write the greatest rock 'n' roll song ever.

That fall, like every weekday morning during the school year, my clock radio, set to 7:00am, woke me up. I always had the station tuned to WNEW-FM in New York. Pulling the covers over my head, I wanted to go back to sleep, but the song on the radio caught my attention. I reluctantly got out of bed, rummaged through the pile of laundry to find my favorite jeans and t-shirt, and gathered my homework scattered on the floor. I cringed as David Cassidy and Bobby Sherman stared back at me from the posters on the wall. Even though I had out-grown my pre-teen celebrity crushes, I had nothing to replace them with.

That was about to change.

As I scrambled to stuff everything into my backpack, I heard the DJ announce the catchy new song I had been listening to. Little did I know, at the time, how that song, and the man behind it, would change my life.

"That was 'Born to Run' by Bruce Springsteen, from Freehold, New Jersey," the DJ announced. At the moment, my life changed

The old posters were soon replaced with Springsteen posters, and within weeks, I had memorized every word to every song on all three of his albums.

As a shy and insecure teenager, I had a hard time connecting with other kids and although Bruce wasn't the answer to all my problems, his music gave me hope and was a catalyst for connecting with other kids, making new friends, and getting out of my own head.

Bruce's small-town-loner-turns-rock-star story offered a glimmer of hope that life might just turn out ok.

In His Own Words

Over the years, I've tried, and failed, to describe Bruce's connection with his audience. The following quotes sum it up nicely.

*'The main thing is to cut down on the distance ... to get as close as possible to the audience ... the whole concept is the people come and they're at the show, well, they're not at the show, **they're in the show**, I'm not only in the show, **I'm at the show**... it's a paradox ... the more popular you are, the further people have to sit away to see you but you're reaching more people ... you gotta work it out somehow.'*
Interview with Dave Herman from WNEW Studios in New York

'You're dealing with the alchemy of yourself and your audience, and that's a swirling, changing experience from moment to moment. I go out and both guide and allow myself to be guided by the audience.

If you can mentally project yourself to the last row, you'll be fine. It's all about making that initial connection with the audience. If you do that, the folks at the back will feel it, the folks in the middle will feel it, the folks at the front will feel it.

I may have [played a song 100 times] but that guy [in the audience] is only hearing it that night. Part of my job is to have a foot on stage and a foot in the audience. To have one ear to the band and one ear to the crowd. If you do that correctly you experience the evening through their ears as well as your own.'
- *Source: The Guardian, @michaelahann, January 12, 2017*

My "Bruce Buddies"

Patty

Patty and I lived in adjacent rooms in college. We quickly discovered our mutual love for playing music while studying. She favored Mick Jagger, and I favored Bruce. Before the first semester ended, that changed. She was converted.

To date, she has attended more shows than I, but every time we see him together, it's an adventure. Thank you, Patty, for being a great friend and partner in crime at all the shows!! My Springsteen journey and life journey would not be the same without you.

Terry

I shared many earlier Springsteen shenanigans with Terry, a friend from high school, and my roommate in college. Terry was goal-oriented, organized and tidy. I was more go-with-the-flow, creative, spontaneous, and messy, and even though we appreciated each other's quirks, sometimes we drove each other crazy.

Nonetheless, she was always a good sport when it came to my obsession with Springsteen. You'll see what I mean in the upcoming stories.

Part 1: Lori's Stories

1979: The Fast Lane, Asbury Park, NJ

In April 1979, I was two months away from graduating high school, and planned to attend Rider University in the fall. Bruce was preparing to go on tour for his fourth studio album, *Darkness on the Edge of Town*.

He frequently showed up, unannounced, at various bars along the Jersey Shore, including the Stone Pony in Asbury Park, which was famous for launching the careers of New Jersey music legends including Jon Bon Jovi, Southside Johnny and the Asbury Jukes, and Bruce.

I was a regular at the Pony on Sunday nights to see my favorite band, Cats on a Smooth Surface. Harry Filkin, Joel Krauss and Bobby Bandiera were in the band. I had a mad crush on Harry, but he was a little older than me so I kept my feelings to myself. Even though we were there to see Cats, Bruce showed up unannounced many times, which was thrilling! Seeing him perform in such a small venue was incredible; even spiritual. His energy and ability to connect with the audience was amazing. Often, he'd just hang out at the bar sipping a beer, and I tried to get up my nerve to approach him, but I had no idea what to say, so I never did. But then, one night, the opportunity presented itself and I was finally able to have a very short but life-changing exchange with Bruce.

In April, 1979, at 1:00 in the morning, some guy at the Stone Pony said Bruce was at the Fast Lane, right down the street. Terry and I grabbed our coats, and RAN to the Fast Lane to see if it was true. Was this the moment I had been waiting for?

We approached the bar, out of breath, adrenaline pumping, and were stopped by the bouncer who checked our ID and informed us of the $2 cover charge. We were out of money, but since it was so late, he let us inside anyway. The place was practically empty, so we figured if Bruce was here earlier, he probably already left. But we were wrong.

I spotted him sitting at the bar, and I froze in my tracks. For some reason, maybe due to the late hour and the fact that there was hardly anyone else in the bar, this felt different than the times I had seen him at the Pony. I got nervous. My stomach was doing flip flops, my palms were sweating, and my heart was beating out of my chest. I could barely breathe. Terry was saying something, but my mind was a million miles away.

I was star-struck. My legs turned to rubber. I could barely think. Should I approach him? Give him a hug? Ask for his autograph? Do nothing? My time ran out because at that moment, he paid for his beer and was on his feet, heading in my direction. For a split second, I thought he was coming towards me to say hello but quickly realized he was heading for the door, which was directly behind me. *He had to pass me to leave!*

Terry said something like, "What should we do? He's coming our way!"

This was my chance. My brain went from being paralyzed to fantasizing about our future life together.

He walked towards me, glanced in my direction, and smiled. I shyly smiled back. He paused, put his hands in his pockets, and instead of continuing to the exit, he came towards me. We'd kiss, fall in love, travel the world together, and live happily ever after. "I wanna know if love is wild..I wanna know if love is real!"

Terry saw the glazed look in my eyes and elbowed me in the ribs. I snapped out of it. Bruce was just a few steps away. I blurted out, "Hi Bruce. My name is Lori. Can I have a kiss?" He stopped, looked me in the eye, smiled, and said, "Sure." *Was my fantasy coming true?*

He leaned towards me and then at the last second, he turned his head and presented his stubble-covered cheek. I gave him a peck, and before I knew it, he was gone. My fantasy was crushed.

But I kissed Bruce Springsteen!! *I kissed Bruce!!*

I gently touched my lips. My brain was exploding. Did this really happen? Terry grabbed my arm, and dragged me outside. Bruce was lingering just outside the door, signing autographs, so I quickly took a photo, and then he was on his way.

I'll never know how I found the nerve to ask for a kiss, but it was a moment I'll never forget, even if the fantasy didn't come true.

1981: Big Man's West, Red Bank, NJ

In the summer of 1981, I was 20 years old. Two years earlier, my mom was diagnosed with ovarian cancer. After enduring chemo treatments, she had a short remission, but the cancer came back.

My grandmother lived with us to help take care of her, and by the end of the summer, my mom was sleeping in a hospital bed in the living room. Despite all the signs that she wasn't getting better, I was in denial. It never occurred to me that she wouldn't survive, because the doctors kept our hopes up. I kept busy, going to work and school and hanging out with friends, but upon reflection, I see staying busy was a coping strategy to avoid facing the truth about her condition.

In addition to all the other things I was doing, Chasing Bruce became an obsession; a welcome escape from the reality I was unable to face.

Going to extremes

In July of 1981, Clarence "Big Man" Clemons, sax player for the E Street Band, opened a nightclub in Red Bank, New Jersey, called Big Man's West. It was a key fixture in the revival of the Jersey Shore music scene in the early 1980s, along with the Stone Pony and The Fast Lane.

On July 11, 1981, Clarence and the Red Bank Rockers were scheduled to play at the club's opening party. Bruce had just finished a six-night run at the Meadowlands and had a few days off before heading to Philadelphia for another five shows, so rumors were flying that Bruce would show up. My friends assumed I had tickets, and asked if I had any extras. But I came up empty handed.

I called the bar to get tickets, but they had sold out immediately.

In those days, there was no StubHub, Facebook, or internet. To get tickets for something like this, you had to know someone, which I didn't. What I did have was determination; so on the day of the show, I convinced Terry to drive to Red Bank with me to try and scalp a ticket. We arrived at 1:00 PM, and were surprised to see that the doors were wide open; the bar was serving lunch. We found a table, ordered lunch, and started formatting a plan.

I whispered to Terry, "Since we're already here, let's just hang out until they open the back bar (where the stage was located). Are you cool with that?"

"Sure! Sounds good to me." she replied.

We weren't sure if Bruce would show up, but either way it would be a great night of music. And then, we had a setback. A staff member walked into the lunch area, clipboard in hand, and announced:

"We're closing soon for a private event, so if your name isn't on this list, you need to leave."

What?? No!! If we leave, we'll never get back in. We had to come up with a plan. It was then that I noticed the rest rooms. The light bulb went off...

"I have an idea! After paying the check, let's hide in the restroom until they start letting people in. It'll probably only be about three or four hours. When they open the doors for everyone else, we'll come out of the bathroom and blend in with the crowd. Brilliant, right?" I gushed.

Terry was horrified. "You can't be serious. I know you like Bruce, but that's going too far. We're not even sure he'll show up. There's no way I'm spending four hours in a bathroom, *just in case*."

After some negotiation, she agreed, but if the bathroom was gross, I promised we'd leave. We paid the bill and as casually as possible, walked into the ladies' room. It wasn't too bad. There were two stalls, one sink, and a mirror. Some graffiti on the walls. We'd survive.

"What if a waitress or staff member comes in to use the bathroom?" Terry asked. "We'll probably get kicked out."

She had a point.

"Let's both go into one of the stalls and take turns standing/squatting on the toilet so just in case someone comes in, they'll only see two feet on the ground." I said.

What was behind this sudden streak of mischief?

Terry rolled her eyes and reluctantly agreed.

It turned out we didn't need to worry about getting caught, because only two women came to use the bathroom during the four hours and didn't even notice that one of the stalls was being "used." We passed the time by reading the silly graffiti on the walls, talking about boys, and listening for clues about what was happening outside.

Back then, we used actual cameras, not phones, to record special moments in our lives. The latest innovation at the time was the compact 110 Instamatic camera. It was convenient to carry around, but the photo quality wasn't great because the film was tiny. But that's all I had, so I tucked the Vivitar in my purse, prepared to document the evening. Little did I know that, 50 years later, those photos would end up in this book, and on the walls of some local art galleries right here in Asbury Park!

Around 6:30, we heard commotion in the hallway as they prepared to open the doors. Later, we learned that fans were lined up around the block all afternoon in the hot July sun while we took turns balancing ourselves on top of a toilet. Neither option was optimal. In any case, it was almost time to implement the exit strategy we had been planning. We had to time it just right. Walk out too soon? Risk getting caught. Wait too long? We wouldn't get a good spot near the stage.

When we heard someone say, "It's time to open the doors," we counted to ten, held our breath, and exited the bathroom. We turned left, towards the back room where the stage was, just steps in front of the crowd pushing through the doors. Perfect timing! A few seconds later, we were standing right up against the stage, front and center. We were in the best position possible!

At this point, we still weren't sure if Bruce would show up, but based on the energy in the room, we were pretty sure he would. I clearly remember Obie Dziedzic, Bruce's "First Fan" and assistant to Steve Van Zandt, was seated on the floor right behind us, along with a couple hundred other fans. And it was hot. My pink cotton t-shirt and purple harem pants were drenched in sweat, and the music hadn't even started yet!. It was the middle of July, and without AC, the bar felt like a sauna.

Our day-long adventure was about to climax as we turned our attention towards the stage. Terry was positioned directly in front of the center microphone; she had THE best spot possible, but as the lights went down, I felt her hands on my shoulders as she switched positions with me. I'll never forget that moment, and the moments that followed. Bruce came out on stage, grabbed the microphone just inches from me, and I was swept away. I sang along to every word, while Bruce's sweat rained down on me like a spring shower. I managed to snap a few photos, which serve as a reminder of one of the best nights of my life.

Clarence Clemons & The Red Bank Rockers were joined on stage by Springsteen and Gary U.S. Bonds for a set that included "Ramrod," "Around and Around," "Summertime Blues," "Jole Blon," "You Can't Sit Down" and "Cadillac Ranch."

As always, Bruce was on fire, as was the crowd. The energy in the room was electric. We all somehow knew this was a very special night. When the music ended, we hung around as long as possible, hoping Bruce might come out and mingle. He never did, but I did get to meet Clarence, and Terry snapped a great photo!

About 12 hours after we arrived, we walked out, past the bathroom, and drove home on cloud 9. Our perseverance paid off.

Winter, 1981

Up to this point, aside from my mom fighting cancer, 1981 was a great year. But once fall rolled around, it turned into the worst year of my life.

In September, I began my junior year of college and my mom began her third round of chemo. The doctors were hopeful this time it would work. Or, at least, that's what they told us, so I went about life as usual: studying, dating, attending classes and parties while away at college. Everything changed when I went home for Thanksgiving to a grim scene. Between the hospital bed in the middle of the living room and the medical equipment piled up in the corner, the family room felt more like a hospital room.

It was obvious that my mom was not getting better, but no one talked about it. I think we all convinced ourselves that if we didn't say it out loud, it wasn't real. I stuffed down my feelings and pretended nothing was wrong. This was typical of my family; we never talked about hard things. We brushed them under the rug.

On Thanksgiving Day, my brother, my dad, and I walked to our neighbor's house to share Thanksgiving dinner, as we had done for the past 15 years. But this time, mom stayed home. She was in no condition to leave the house and had no appetite. She was thin as a rail, and had lost all her hair..

Thanksgiving dinner was somber. We tried to act normal, but failed to hide our despair. Between passing the turkey and mashed potatoes, there were long moments of awkward silence.

Thanksgiving 1981 was the last time I saw my mom.

She was a shining light in the world. One of the few children who survived the Holocaust, she migrated to this country at the age of 12, not knowing one word of English, with my grandparents and my aunt. They eventually landed in Freehold, where my mom thrived and eventually met and married my dad. They led a quiet but full life surrounded by friends and family.

Two weeks after Thanksgiving, I was back at school, when a pounding on my dorm room door jolted me awake at 6am.

I muddled through the rest of junior year in a fog of grief, distracting myself with school and work, but for a very long time, the world felt gray, empty, and devoid of meaning. I miss her to this day.

1995: Ghost of Tom Joad Tour

In 1995, Bruce released *The Ghost of Tom Joad*, and embarked on his first worldwide solo tour, performing in small halls and theaters. He traveled light with just a technician and a sound engineer.

Patty was living in California, and I was living in Maryland. Although we were both married at this point, we left our husbands at home, and met up in Rosemont, IL to see Bruce.

This tour wasn't typical.

Jon Pareles of The New York Times said that Springsteen *'has taken his music to an extreme, a depressive view of tedious, unending woe.'* Greg Kot of the Chicago Tribune wrote, *'In contrast to past tours, which have been celebratory events tinged by introspection, Springsteen brought a sobering sense of solitude to these shows.'*

These shows were different from the famous, four-hour, high-energy performances with the E Street Band. *The Ghost of Tom Joad* performances were dark and quiet, and Springsteen even asked the audience for silence on occasion. When performing songs from other albums, like *Born in the USA*, they were also presented as mellow rearrangements.

On December 3rd, the day of the show, we checked into our hotel and headed to the lobby to play Scrabble. I had upgraded from my 110-Vivitar Instamatic to a Kodak 35mm throw-away version. In the middle of the second Scrabble game, we noticed some commotion by the front door of the hotel. "Oh my God, it's him! It's Bruce!" Patty said, jumping out of her chair, knocking all the Scrabble pieces on the floor, and almost fell head first as she charged toward the crowd. I was right behind her, camera in hand.

He walked right by us, sporting a ponytail and carrying his guitar, accompanied by one security guy. We knew we only had a minute to catch a glimpse up close so we elbowed our way to the inner circle, and I snapped a few very bad photos.

In a flash, he was inside the elevator and then was gone. We fantasized about finding his room and stalking him. We nixed that idea, but assumed he'd have to go through the lobby on his way out to the venue in a couple of hours, so we bolted back up to our room, gathered everything we needed for the show, and parked ourselves in the lobby for the next few hours. He never showed up. We figured he probably took the service elevator. Damn.

At around 6:00 p.m., we headed to the Rosemont Theater, a 4400-seat venue, quite different from the 20,000-seat stadium we were used to. As we sunk into the soft, velvet seats and took in the beautiful, ornate decor, we knew this would be a special night. I felt excited but calm at the same time.

When the lights went down, the audience was up on their feet, welcoming Bruce to the stage with five minutes of yelling, clapping, and shouts of BRUUUUUUUCE, which, to the first-timer, sounds like "booooo." Once everyone settled down, we were treated to an epic night of music. The acoustics were perfect, and instead of the typical, high-energy, loud and quite active performance, this version of Bruce was quiet but just as powerful.

It's impossible to compare the raw and powerful performance of Bruce playing solo with the rousing, high-energy, rock-n-roll extravaganzas we were used to. His voice and energy filled the theater as he took us on a journey filled with despair, hope, and dreams. It was intimate and moving.

Bruce described his thoughts about the album and the tour.

"The Ghost of Tom Joad was the result of a decade-long inner conversation I'd been having with myself after the

success of Born in the USA. That debate centered on a single question: Where does a rich man belong? If it was true that it's 'easier for a camel to go through the eye of a needle than for a rich man to enter the kingdom of God,' I wouldn't be walking through those pearly gates any time soon, but that was ok; there was still plenty of work to be done down here on Earth. That was the premise of The Ghost of Tom Joad. What is the work for us to do in our short time here?" -Bruce Springsteen

Without the E Street Band, it was pure Bruce, and one of the most memorable shows of the 50+ I have attended. Seeing him, alone, on stage with just his guitar, piano and harmonica, was mind-blowing. Springsteen on Broadway was the next best thing. Afterwards, Patty and I went back to the hotel and parked ourselves back in the lobby, hoping we'd catch another glimpse of Bruce, but we gave up around midnight.

Over the next few years, I attended shows in 1999, 2002, and 2003, which were all amazing, but there weren't any interesting stories to tell.

2007: Magic Tour, Oakland Arena

In 2007, we lived in Maryland, and my kids were 9 and 12. Our days were filled with getting the boys off to school, going to work, attending soccer and basketball games and Boy Scout meetings. It was a busy but fun time. In the fall of that year, Bruce was preparing for the The Magic Tour.

The Magic Tour:
- Was one of the biggest tours of the year
- Won the 2008 Billboard Touring Awards for Top Tour, Top Draw, and Top Manager (for Jon Landau)
- Had the second-highest gross worldwide for 2008 in Billboard's rankings, with $204.5 million
- Had the sixth-highest gross for 2008 at $69.3 million
- Over its two years, the Magic Tour grossed more than $235 million.

-Wikipedia

Despite the tour's success, there was a dark side. Dan Federici, the band's organist, lost his battle with cancer on April 17, 2008. Federici's passing reminded us of how the years were flying by. Both the band members AND the fans were getting older. In the early days, we didn't think twice about spending the good part of the day on our feet, waiting in line, checking in every hour or so to keep our place in line so we could get into the pit. But these days, that was less appealing, especially for this tour, as Patty was having issues with her neck and was in a lot of pain.

We had tickets for the Oakland show on October 25th. Due to her neck issues, I tried to convince Patty to sell the GA tickets and get seats instead, but she's a trooper (aka stubborn) and was determined to push through. We arrived at the Oakland Arena around 2:00 to get our wristbands for the pit lottery.

It was a bit of a walk from our parking spot to where the GA ticket holders were lined up, and since Patty was hurting, we took our time. As she hobbled through the parking lot, we chatted with a couple of guys heading in the same direction.

"What's going on with your friend? She doesn't look so good." John whispered to me, nodding towards Patty.

"She has something going on with her neck, but she'll be ok." I said.

They wished us luck and then walked ahead to the designated area.

Ten minutes later, we got our numbers. We tried to find a comfortable place to hang out for the next couple of hours, but given we were in a parking lot, that was pretty much impossible.

About an hour later, the guys we met earlier found us.

"How are you feeling, Patty?" said John.

"Pretty much the same," she replied.

"We want to show you something. Follow us," he said.

We looked at each other, shrugged our shoulders, and followed them towards the front of the line.

John said, "Patty and Lori, this is Jerry, the head of security."

"Hello." we said.

We wondered what was going on. Were we in trouble? Did we do something wrong? Why did they call us over here?

Without any explanation, Jerry instructed us to stand in a separate area until it was time to go inside.

He pointed to a group of people near the front of the line, behind the security partition. We were confused at first. One guy was in a wheelchair, another was on crutches, and another woman, with a companion, appeared to have a vision impairment. We were grouped with the physically challenged. What did this mean? Would we still have a shot at getting to the front of the pit? Or would we be placed in a special area further away from the stage? We were a little concerned.

Our questions were answered soon enough. Jerry explained to us that the physically challenged group would be let in BEFORE EVERYONE ELSE! We didn't even have to participate in the lottery for the pit! We were in!

We spent the next hour chatting with Jerry about what it was like being on tour with the Boss. He was a really nice guy and had some great stories to tell.

At around 6:00, the staff prepared to open the doors. After a very long day of waiting around, we were ready. When the doors opened, we had plenty of time to make our way to the stage, but walked quickly and chose our spot. *Right up front!* Again! It felt good to sit down after standing in line for almost four hours, even though it was on the cold, cement floor.

For the next four hours, the music served as medicine for both of us.

2007: Magic Tour, Part 2, Washington DC

One of the fun things about having kids is sharing your passions with them. In 2007, Jason was 12 and it was time to bring him to a live show. He started listening to Springsteen in the womb, so he was excited, and I was thrilled that he wanted to attend.

I was curious to see his response because for me, it's more of a spiritual experience than a rock concert. Even though a Springsteen show might never hold the same depth of meaning for him as it does for me, he had a great time.

Bruce was scheduled to play in DC the following night at the Verizon Center, about six blocks from my office. I couldn't stay away, even though I didn't have tickets.

Yet.

I arrived at around 5pm. People were milling around, waiting for the pit lottery. I ran into one of the security guys that Patty and I met the week before in Oakland.

"Hi!" I said. "Do you remember me from two weeks ago at the Oakland show?"

"Sure! How's your friend feeling?" he said.

"Better, thanks," I replied.

"Do you have tickets for the show tonight?" he asked.

"No, I just came by to see what was going on."

He reached into his pocket and pulled out a ticket.

"If you're interested, I have an extra! It's an assigned seat, but I can also give you a wristband for the pit in case you want to go down there. You'll probably be towards the back since they already let in the pit group, " he said.

Wow. How could I pass this up?? A seat AND a pit ticket?? I was tempted, but I had responsibilities! WHo would make the kids dinner? My husband was working late that night so it was all on me.

"Give me a minute; I need to make a phone call."

I pulled out my phone and called my younger son, Kevin.

"Hi. How was school?" I asked.
"Fine. When are you coming home from work?" he asked.
"Well, that's why I'm calling. Springsteen is playing in DC tonight, and I was offered a ticket, but I didn't want to leave you guys to fend for yourselves for dinner since Dad might be home late," I explained.
"You have to go! You love Bruce! He's your favorite! We'll just make peanut butter and jelly. We'll be fine!" he said.
I was so relieved. "Are you sure? Ok, then, I will!"
"Have fun!" he said, and we hung up.
I found an ATM, got the $100, and handed it over.
"Here you go," he said as he handed me a ticket and placed a band on my wrist.
"Thank you! I'm so excited!" I gushed.
"You're welcome. Have a great time!" he exclaimed.

I walked to the main entrance and waited. A few minutes later, they opened the doors, scanned my ticket, and I was in. I walked straight ahead towards the stairs that led down to the floor area. I could see the entire floor section, and to my surprise, it was empty. My eyes were drawn across the floor to the opposite side, towards the back, where I could see the "pit people" waiting to be let in.

My mind went on overdrive. I had a pit wristband! If I could get down there before the rest of the crowd, I could get up front! I bolted down the stairs, showed my wristband to the usher, and fast-walked towards the stage. At that moment, they let in the pit crowd, but I was ahead of them. I found my spot on the floor, center stage, and was soon surrounded by all the others.

It wasn't quite the same without Patty by my side, but I made the best of it. My favorite song that night was *Thunder Road*, missing from the previous night's setlist. There's a moment in the first part of the song when the audience sings a verse, and it gives me goosebumps.

Every.
Single.
Time.

2012: The Wrecking Ball Tour, Anaheim, CA

In the fall of 2012, I was teaching art classes in San Jose, California, and Patty was busy with her career and family.

Bruce's 17th album, *Wrecking Ball*, was released in March 2012. The tour that followed carried with it the ghost of Clarence Clemens, Bruce's sidekick and friend since the beginning, who passed away in June of 2011. To fill the gap, Bruce added a horn section, some backup vocals, and a new sax player, Jake Clemens, Clarence's nephew.

The Scheming Begins

As I packed for the show in Los Angeles, I thought about how we could maximize our chances of getting into the pit in case we didn't get a good number. After being in the front of the pit, anything less just wouldn't do. The rule-breaker in me wondered how hard it would be to make fake wristbands if we didn't make the cut. I decided to bring along some supplies:

- scotch tape
- masking tape
- variety of colored markers
- selection of sample wristbands in all colors
- black sharpie

In those days, wristbands were low-tech, so with the right tools, it was possible to replicate them, especially once the lights went down, when it's harder to tell the fake from the real ones. I ordered some sample wrist bands online, in all colors, and brought along the other supplies as a backup. If we didn't get chosen for the pit, we were prepared for Plan B.

Getting into the pit is a long and exhausting process.

Step 1: Purchase a GA ticket (hard to get).

Step 2: Arrive at the venue early to receive a number. The number determines your place in line for the lottery.

Step 3: At 4:00, line up according to your number. A number gets picked out of a hat, and that becomes number "1." The next 500 people line up behind that person. If you don't make the cut, then you end up behind the partition which is about ⅓ of the way back on the floor. It wasn't our lucky day. We didn't make the cut.

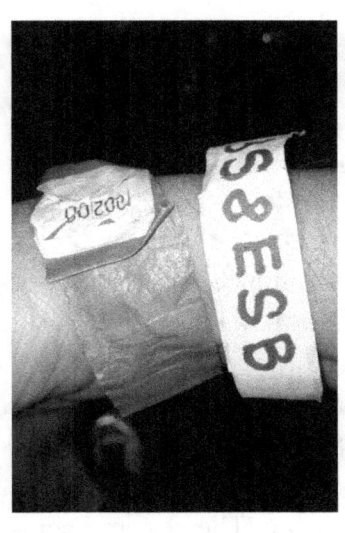

We had a couple of hours to kill, so we went to dinner across the street. At the restaurant, the napkin rings, made with white paper, were the size of a wristband, so we carefully stashed them in our bag.

Once inside the arena, we ended up right behind the platform, a great position to see Bruce up close when he made his way there later in the show.

Still, we were determined to get into the pit. I spotted a girl with a pit wristband. It was neon yellow, with the letters BS&ESB (Bruce Springsteen and the E Street Band) written in black.

I dug through my backpack and realized I did NOT bring a neon yellow highlighter. My heart sank. Now what? Then we noticed the two guys sitting near us.

"Check out that guy's shirt pocket. Is that a yellow highlighter?" Patty said.

It was! Now, we just had to figure out how to borrow (or steal) it.

"Excuse me, my name is Lori, and this is Patty. Is this your first show?" I said, trying to make friends before swooping in with what I really wanted.

"Hi. Yes, this is our first show." the guy said hesitantly. They weren't forthcoming or friendly and showed no interest in conversing with us.

I took the direct approach.

"Would you mind if I borrowed your highlighter for a minute?" I asked.

With a puzzled look, he shrugged his shoulders, pulled it out of his pocket, and handed it over. "Thanks," I said.

I colored the white napkin rings with the highlighter, discreetly, INSIDE my backpack.

After returning the highlighter I wrote BS&ESB, in black, on each one. Patty taped mine together with masking tape, and I used scotch tape for hers.

The whole time, we were observing the "pit police." As each person walked by, they showed their wristband and then moved forward into the crowd. We waited until the lights went down, took a deep breath and made our way to the pit entrance. My heart was beating, and my palms were sweating. Would they kick us out if we got caught? Was it worth taking the chance? Maybe we should just stay where we were; it was a pretty good spot. There was no turning back now! I approached the security guy, I raised my arm, and kept walking, with Patty right behind me.

And then, our whole plan almost blew up. The next moments felt like slow motion. We didn't know about the *second* wristband checker. Instead of visually checking the wristband, this guy stuck his finger under the band and gave a tug. The REAL wristbands held up with no problem because they were made of plastic and had a reinforced closure. But ours were flimsy paper that likely would not hold.

I was freaking out, and held my breath as he tugged…it held together!! What a relief. I could breathe again. As I moved forward towards the pit, I turned to check on Patty. When he tugged on her band, it tore open and fell off!! She waved me on, "Keep going!" she yelled. I thought, there's no way I'm leaving her behind! But she didn't stop. She kept coming towards me, because the security guy's attention was focused on the girl *behind* Patty who was also trying to sneak into the pit, but *without a wristband at all*! We kept moving and were quickly swallowed up in the crowd before the guy had a chance to chase us. Lesson learned: use masking tape instead of scotch tape.

2016: The River Tour #2

The River Tour was a celebration of Springsteen's 2015 release of *The Ties That Bind: The River Collection* box set and the 35th anniversary of Springsteen's 1980 album, *The River.* It was the top-grossing worldwide tour of 2016.

The original *River Tour* shows, from October 1980 through September 1981, averaged four hours, solidifying Bruce and the E Street Band's reputation for marathon shows.

This was the first time Springsteen performed an entire album from start to finish. The show on September 7, 2016, at Citizens Bank Park in Philadelphia, ran four hours and four minutes, marking it as Springsteen's longest show ever performed in the United States.

During this time. I was living in Northern California, about two hours south of Patty. My husband and I were remodeling our house, a stressful endeavor, and I needed a distraction. Bruce to the rescue!! Patty and I scored two GA tickets for March 15th at the LA Sports Arena, and I got tickets for the Oakland Arena on March 13th so I could bring my younger son, Kevin. It was time to introduce him to a live Bruce show. He loved it!

2023: Portland, Oregon

A lot happened between 2016 and 2023. First there was COVID, and then I got divorced and moved back to my home state of New Jersey, just one mile from Asbury Park. It was a challenging time, but I was ready for a new start.

During COVID, Bruce kept busy, broadcasting a SIRIUS XM series called 'From My Home to Yours,' and then 'Letter to You Radio,' leading up to the release of the *Letter to You* album in October, 2020. Bruce also made a number of virtual appearances during this time, including a Stand Up for Heroes benefit, and appeared on *Saturday Night Live* as the musical guest.

Bruce resumed his *Springsteen on Broadway* run in June of 2021. In January 2023, he began rehearsals for the upcoming 2023–2025 Tour. After such a long and difficult break, everyone was itching for music, community, and Bruce!

Patty scored two GA tickets for the Portland show in February 2025, but her husband couldn't attend, so she offered me the ticket. Since I already had two seats for me and my friend Mary and wasn't up for standing around all day for the pit lottery, I declined, and she sold it. Later, I learned they changed the system. No more lottery. Instead, they simply sold pit tickets right off the bat.

Had I known, I would have bought Patty's extra ticket, a guaranteed spot in the pit.

Still, there was the issue of who gets to enter the arena first. Was there an official process? First-come first-served?

Here's how it went. A fan showed up early and wrote numbers on ticket-holders' hands as they arrived throughout the day, and then later, closer to showtime, everyone lined up according to their number. Simple.

Patty got her number, and I got one too, just in case another ticket fell from the sky.

I searched online, but wasn't willing to shell out $1000. But at around 5:30, a ticket showed up for $400, so I bought it!

We lined up as instructed and waited for the doors to open. I was so excited about being in the pit with Patty, just like old times! And just like old times, we were nervous about getting a good spot.

The process was simple enough. One by one, we'd go through security and follow the person in front of us until we all got down to the pit. But it didn't go as planned.

The line was moving steadily until the guy in front of us had an issue with his ticket. But the group ahead of him kept moving, so once we passed through the screeners, we didn't know which way to go. We were in a panic because we might lose the chance to get RIGHT UP FRONT!! My heart was beating fast as the adrenaline kicked in.

"Which way should we go?" Patty said in a panic.

I asked an usher, "How do we get to the floor area?" she shrugged and shook her head. "I'm sorry, I have no idea." Fuck.

"Let's try this way!!" I said.

We ran to the left for a minute but didn't see anyone from our group. I spotted another usher.

"Where's the entrance to the floor area?" I asked, breathless and shaking.

He pointed and said, "Take that elevator down one floor, and you'll be there."

We raced to the elevator, took it down one floor, and then scrambled to figure out where to go.

We were at the back of the floor area. But where was everyone else? We spotted the line of fans snaking up the steps on the other side of the arena. Ushers were checking tickets and giving out pit wristbands, but the line moved slowly and people were getting impatient, causing the ushers to get annoyed which slowed things down even more.

In the midst of the chaos, we took a deep breath and approached calmly. We smiled, showed our tickets, held out our arms, and once branded with the wristband, we bolted towards the stage. There were about 25 people down there, so we ended up in the same spot had we been able to follow the line as planned.

We were slightly to the right of Bruce's microphone. Soon, Bruce took the stage and played many of my favorites: *No Surrender, Out in the Street, E Street Shuffle, Backstreets, and She's the One.* He closed with his standard, *I'll See You in my Dreams*, and we left feeling elated, as always.

Lori and Patty

2024: Sea Hear Now Festival, Asbury Park, NJ

I moved back to the Jersey Shore just in time to attend the Sea Hear Now music Festival in Asbury Park. For the first time since the festival started in 2018, Bruce Springsteen was the headliner! I rode my bike over to Asbury for this once-in-a-lifetime opportunity to see Bruce perform in the town where he wrote many of his earlier songs, and sing about the very beach and boardwalk where we stood.

My cousin Keri joined me. It was her first time seeing Bruce live. Bruce took the stage at dusk, with over 35,000 fans in attendance. The beach and the boardwalk were packed. The air was electric. A cluster of boats were rocking in the rough surf just off shore. Keri and I were giddy with anticipation.

After kicking off with "Lonesome Day", Bruce said, "I wrote this song about 500 yards north of here on Loch Arbor Beach. We haven't played it in a long fucking time. We got a lot of stuff we haven't played in a long fucking time. Let's see how we do."

In this fan's humble opinion, they did pretty good.

My concert history

Date	Location	Tour/Performance
9/21/79	Madison Square Garden	No Nukes concert
10/79	The Fast Lane (first kiss)	Performed with Ellen Shipley
12/9/80	Spectrum	River Tour
1981	Stone Pony	The photo of Bruce and I
7/11/81	Big Man's West	Ramrod / Around and Around / Summertime Blues / You Can't Sit Down / Cadillac Ranch
7/15/81	Philadelphia Spectrum	River Tour
4/10/82	Big Man's West	Lucielle/Jersey Girl/Jole Blon/Twist and Shout
8/8/84	Meadowlands	Born in the USA Tour
8/16/84	Meadowlands	Born in the USA Tour
8/19/84	Meadowlands	Born in the USA Tour
8/26/84	Capital Centre	Born in the USA Tour
8/21/85	Meadowlands	Born in the USA Tour
5/19/88	Madison Square Garden	Tunnel of Love
5/22/88	Madison Square Garden	Tunnel of Love
8/25/92	Capital Centre	92-93 World Tour
12/3/95	Rosemont Theatre	Tom Joad Tour
7/26/99	Continental Arena	Reunion Tour
10/25/99	Oakland Arena, CA	Reunion Tour

10/26/99	Oakland Arena, CA	Reunion Tour
10/28/99	Oakland Arena, CA	Reunion Tour
8/7/02	Continental Arena	The Rising Tour
8/27/02	Compaq center	The Rising Tour
8/16/03	Pac Bell Park, SF	The Rising Tour
9/10/04	Palace of Fine Arts, SF	Springsteen presents Sean Penn with the Steinbeck Award
11/13/05	Boardwalk Hall, A/C	Solo acoustic, Devils and Dust
11/9/05	Wachovia Spectrum	Solo acoustic, Devils and Dust
10/25/07	Oracle Arena	Magic Tour
11/11/07	Verizon Center, DC with Jason	Magic Tour
11/12/07	Verizon Center, DC	Magic Tour
4/1/09	HP Pavilion, San Jose	Working on a Dream Tour
4/24/12	HP Pavilion, San Jose	Wrecking Ball Tour
4/4/12	Honda Center	Wrecking Ball Tour
11/30/12	Oakland Arena	Wrecking Ball Tour
3/13/16	Oakland Arena with Kevin	The River Tour
3/15/16	LA Stadium	The River Tour
4/17/18	Walter Kerr Theater, NYC	Bruce on Broadway
2/25/23	Portland, OR	2023/2024 tour
11/22/24	Vancouver, CA	2023/2024 tour

Part 2: Stories from other fans

When I began this project, I signed up for a memoir writing class through Project Write Now and began submitting chapters for review. The feedback was encouraging and motivated me to keep going. Our instructor, Mark, was also a Springsteen fan and suggested that I reach out to other fans who might be interested in telling their stories. I took his advice and received a few submissions.

A lifetime fan meets Bruce: Jeffrey Carhart – Toronto

As you may know, Bruce Springsteen loves baseball. He's written songs and made videos about it and has been photographed in attendance at Major League Baseball games. In thinking about the start of this brief essay about my relationship with Bruce Springsteen, I remembered that Joe Carter [a World Series hero for the Toronto Blue Jays] once said that he 'has a love affair with Canada that just will not die.' That description certainly conveys some of how I feel about Bruce and what he has done for me.

I will sketch out, briefly, some highlights and milestones from that long, beautiful relationship – including the day when I met Bruce in 2016 - which has helped me enormously.

In the mid-1970's, I was approaching graduation from high school in Winnipeg, Manitoba. (Music fans might already know that Winnipeg is the home of Neil Young who relocated from Ontario in his early childhood, Randy Bachman and Burton Cummings. I can't recall the exact number, but I once read an article in the Winnipeg media suggesting that, when you included all of their different groups and solo projects, these three guys have sold around 150 million records.)

Growing up, our small household was the opposite of affluent; we didn't have much. Vacations were something other people took and told you about. However, I remember one small luxury that we had and that I appreciated – a subscription to *Newsweek* magazine. One day an issue was in the mailbox with Bruce on the cover. I wondered, who was this guy?

Since then, I have often pondered the fact that in the pre-internet world, *Newsweek* (and *Time*) magazines were the first time that many of us outside the Philadelphia-New York corridor had heard of Bruce. I must have read that article twenty times and quickly got my first copy of *Born to Run*. How many copies have you owned? Dating myself, my numerous editions included an eight-track cassette. I still have a large amount of my original Bruce paraphernalia – for example, a 1978 "The Boss is Back" concert

T-shirt in excellent condition - but somehow, that Eight Track got lost along the way.

I also devoured *Greetings from Asbury Park, N.J.* and *The Wild, the Innocent & the E Street Shuffle.*

With Bruce now along for the ride, I was on the road to the rest of my life. I moved to Ontario for university at Queen's and Law School at Western and then moved to Toronto (where I have lived and worked ever since) in 1982. The journey has also included – along with all the hard, painful stuff, a beautiful marriage to my wife Kathe, two great sons, some professional success (as a member of some great teams – which was always my system for attaining any success I ever had at sports), some great travelling…and Bruce – lots and lots of Bruce.

I'll share some highlights and milestones of this great journey, which "goes until it ends." (That's a Bruce quotation reference – if you know, you know.)

Among other things, when I was at Queen's and Western in the late 70's and early 80's:

- I saw my first Bruce concert in 1977 at the old Maple Leaf Gardens (what was known as the Chicken Scratch Tour – when his lawsuit with Mike Appel kept him out of the recording studio.)
- I lived with five other guys at Queen's ($350 a month for the whole house.) We had house T-shirts made with our address on the front and "Prove It All Night" on the back. We wore them around campus.
- I started reading everything I could get my hands on in those pre-internet days. I could barely wait for the next record after *Born to Run.* When *Darkness on the Edge of Town* was finally released, I was in the store on Day 1 and ran back to my house to play it on my Pioneer turntable. It fulfilled all my hopes and expectations and is still my favourite single record.

At the time, it seemed like many famous people wanted to "get away" from their "old life," particularly if it was a Spartan, working-class one, and no one wanted to talk about that life. In contrast, Bruce confronted it all – good & bad - in fascinating and powerful terms. I felt as if he was expressing the things close to my heart as great art. I felt like he was talking *directly to me*. It was extremely powerful and still is.

I saw a couple of the legendary 1978 *Darkness on the Edge of Town* Tour shows:
- The old Syracuse War Memorial Arena: As I recall, I sent away for the tickets in the mail with a check – without specifying a seat and with no color-coded "seating plan." My friend and I ended up in the middle of the seventh row. It remains the closest to the stage that I have ever been. In those days, Bruce waded into the crowd during *Spirit in the Night,* and he was very close to us.
- Maple Leaf Gardens in Toronto: I brought several friends from Queen's on the basis of my eloquent statement, "you have to see this guy!" Over the decades, I have often tried to go with someone who has never seen him before. I love looking at their eyes as the first few songs unfold.

I live in the hope that one or both of those shows may show up on the official Nugs website someday – along with the other shows from that 1978 Tour that have been officially released.

I enjoyed seeing Bruce perform his first big hit, "Hungry Heart," after writing so many for other artists at the River Tour show at Maple Leaf Gardens.

Over the years, I have seen around 50 Springsteen shows. Most were in Toronto, including the old Exhibition Stadium, the SkyDome, (now the Rogers Centre), and the Air Canada Centre (now the Scotiabank Arena.)

During my first year as a full-time lawyer in the mid-80s, I took a road trip to Asbury Park with a friend in my red Plymouth Duster with about 200,000 miles on its great "Slant 6" engine. The plan was to visit New York, a first time for both of us. As we approached our destination, I said emphatically, "if we are this close, we are going to Asbury Park." We also went to Bruce's hometown, and I was starstruck, sitting in a diner in Freehold.

As the years passed, I purchased and listened to every record when it was released, and saw at least one or two shows on each tour. I always wanted to know what Bruce was talking about. He has never released a record without at least a few devastatingly great songs that I listened to hundreds of times. He never disappointed or failed to give me a lift. Along the way, my concert-going came to include other members of the E Street Band:

- In March of 1984, I saw Clarence Clemons & The Red Bank Rockers at the legendary El Mocambo Bar in Toronto – and met Clarence. Looking back at my autographed ticket from that night, it strikes me that the date was about three months before the release of *Born in the USA,* which changed all of their lives. What I wouldn't give to speak with Clarence again – to ask him one question: On that evening in March of 1984, did he have any idea how massive the *Born in the USA* record would soon be? I felt some powerful emotions seeing Jake Clemons and his band decades later at the Cadillac Lounge Bar in Toronto.
- Nils Lofgren with Cindy Mizelle and the rest of his great band at the City Winery in New York.
- Little Steven and the Disciples of Soul - both in Toronto – where the live version of Working Class Hero that was subsequently released on a CD and Blu-Ray was recorded, and in Red Bank, New Jersey - where footage for the awesome *Stevie Van Zandt: Disciple* HBO documentary was filmed.

Without planning to, I attended two somewhat "famous" Bruce Springsteen and the E Street Band shows.

In the fall of 2003, we saw Bruce's concert at the SkyDome which took place a few days after Warren Zevon passed away. We assumed the first song would be a full-band rock song featuring a Clarence sax solo. Yet, as only Bruce could do, he came out with an acoustic guitar and spoke powerfully about Warren before going into Warren's beautiful song, 'My Ride's Here.' That recording ended up on the great Warren Zevon tribute record *Enjoy Every Sandwich*. It's not the best quality, but there's a great video on YouTube.

In the 2010s, my friend and I drove to Hamilton, Ontario. That show featured an unforgettable moment when a young fellow in the audience held up a sign for 'I'm Going Down.' The sign included information that he had just broken up with his girlfriend. Bruce brought him up on stage and gave him a hug. Among other things, he said, "Don't worry, man, I've been dumped lots of times...(perfect pause) although they're regretting it now!" To my surprise, the full moment was captured in the great Ridley Scott film *Springsteen & I*.

Through perseverance and some luck ("when it comes to luck, you make your own"), I have met many members of the E Street Band. I mentioned meeting Clarence Clemons. I have also met

Max Weinberg (at the University of Toronto), Nils Lofgren (in New Jersey and New York), Gary Tallent (in New Jersey and Toronto), Curtis King (in Toronto) and Anthony Almonte (in Toronto).

In late October, 2016, I met Bruce himself. It was the only Canadian appearance on his book tour for *Born to Run*, and I was able - in my "just don't give up" manner - to get my hands on one of the few tickets for the event at the Indigo Book Store in Yorkville, Toronto. Here is the photographic evidence.

I knew that time was short, so I said to myself, as I neared the front of the line, "just keep it simple."

As I approached, Bruce gave me one of those great looks you sometimes see in concert when he picks someone in the audience; I stuck out my hand and said, "Bruce, I've seen you about 35 times." He responded in his classic New Jersey rasp, "ah…that's good…" We turned to the woman with my camera, and at exactly the right moment, he added, "that's really good!" That timing produced the two spontaneous smiles just as she snapped the picture. I have no memory of putting my arm around him – but obviously I did.

We exchanged a few more words, including him saying "thanks" to me; quite surreal - and then it was over. I remember several exchanges with friends about the picture, including:

- The caption should be, "Finally, a real fan…"
- Another friend told me that he loves the picture and refers to it when work pressures are hard because it makes him happy. Hearing that makes *me* happy because I have taken so many terrible pictures in my life (the kind where you reach for the delete button as quickly as possible) but it feels as if, at that moment, God said, "you know what? I'm going to give you this one."

I left the Indigo store and went on with my life and endless Springsteen journey. As part of that multi-faceted journey, I have read numerous "E Street books" - and even contributed to some of them. I have my name in three (so far):

- Frank Stefanko - *Further Up the Road* - Frank's stupendous photography is a wonderful thing. So are his stories.
- Barry Schneier - *Bruce Springsteen: Rock and Roll Future* – a beautiful look back at the May 9, 1974 performance at Harvard University, inspiring Jon Landau to write his article with the famous line, "I saw rock and roll future and its name is Bruce Springsteen" which started the business relationship and friendship between Jon and Bruce. Barry was the only

photographer there that night, and he was the only one who was needed.
- Robert Lawson - *Solidarity Forever: The Art and Soul of Stevie Van Zandt*. This terrific book takes a detailed look at Steven's music.

I strongly recommend each of those books.

I made a second trip to Asbury Park – this time with Kathe – in 2017. We stayed at the Empress Hotel, captured in the photograph on the 'Hungry Heart' single. We went on Stan Goldstein and Jean Mikle's wonderful tour for several hours, and enjoyed the hip restaurants that were not there in the mid-80's. We still talk about that trip.

With the onset of the COVID in 2020 – when many of us were suddenly at home, alone, in front of our computers - I participated more in social media, including some Springsteen pages and groups. That's where I found out about this book! I have made good "Bruce friends" around the world, including in Canada, the U.S., Japan, France, Israel, Australia, England, Finland, The Netherlands, Brazil and elsewhere. As all Bruce people know, you only need to make a comment or two back and forth with someone to recognize that E Street bond – no matter how many "miles in between" there may be. That bond is powerful, real and wonderful.

I have steadily attended concerts since 1977. As noted, most have been in Toronto or Hamilton, but during every decade since the 70s, I have made at least one road trip to see Bruce somewhere in the U.S. – Chicago, Detroit (twice – slightly more than 40 years apart), Cleveland, Buffalo, Rochester, Syracuse and (only once) New Jersey (at the old Giants Stadium, where we made an appearance in an E Street Lounge).

Thanks to social media, I have come to know a number of people around the world who leave my 50-ish shows in the dust. I recently met another lawyer in Toronto who has been to over 100 shows.

I mentioned my wife, Kathe. It is no overstatement to say that Kathe and Bruce (in that order) have gotten me through life. Very simply, I owe them an enormous debt.

Bruce has helped me face up to the challenges and "the pain that living brings." I know of Bruce's struggles with depression. I sat up in my chair the first time I heard – and read the lyrics to - "Living Proof" on the *Lucky Town* album in the early 90s. I remember being a bit stunned to hear the coolest guy in the world sing about burning out traces of his past self. When journalists around the world started talking about his battles with depression after *Born to Run* came out in 2016, my immediate reaction was, 'hey man, I've known about that since the *Lucky Town* album more than 20 years ago…'

I keep moving forward (to the "next there," as the great Canadian Ken Dryden has said). In late 2024, we attended both concerts in Toronto, with a couple who had never seen him before. They loved it.

A Journey from Liverpool to Freehold - Phil Beard

Little did I know how my first year of retirement would go. I first heard and fell in love with the music of Bruce Springsteen in April 1976, at the age of 23. Since then, Bruce has been the soundtrack to my life, and as each year passes, his music sinks a bit deeper into my soul.

The first one

My first live Springsteen experience was at Wembley Arena in London for the original *River Tour* in 1981. Since then, I have attended 62 nights of joy and raw emotion at shows all around the world, where I am lost in the stars for a moment in time. I am truly thankful and treasure every moment of the shows I have been fortunate enough to attend. The memories are etched in my mind forever and revisited over and over, thanks to the magic of bootlegging and the gift of official downloads.

Forty years later, at the age of 63, my wife Eileen and I are still on this journey. Her passion and commitment have always been infinite, no questions asked. (Thanks Ei).

We retired in October and little did we know how our well-earned retirement fund was about to be considerably plundered.

With the announcement of the American *River 2016 Tour*, we choose to attend Washington, DC and Newark. We scored two GA tickets for the Washington DC show but got shut out for Newark. This was disappointing, but we decided to pony up the cash and found great seats next to the stage.

We were ready, tickets in hand, looking forward to seeing and hearing the entire *River* album once again.

In the pit at The Verizon Center, Washington DC
With My Soul Sister, My Springsteen Buddy, My Wife, Ei

Washington was our first indoor pit experience in North America. That afternoon, we got our wristband numbers 40 and 41, and the number 10 was drawn in the lottery, so we were in! It was awesome being so close to all the action on stage and seeing the expression on Bruce's face. What a show! It was an epic journey from the opening chords of "The Ties That Bind" to the final refrain of "Wreck on the Highway," where Bruce says, "Well, the subtext of *The River* was time, time slippin' away and how once you entered adult life, the clock starts ticking, and you realise you have a limited amount of time to do your work and raise your family and try and do something good" – so true.

New Jersey, Bruuuuuuce!
Next, it was the Prudential Center in Newark for a totally different experience. We got to meet Steve Van Zandt before the show and had a conversation about his music soundtrack for Lillehammer and his choice of coupling "A Salty Dog" by Procol Harum for Bruce's scene in the final episode; "Perfect," he said. He was very proud of this and had been trying for five "f**#*# years" to get them into the Rock and Roll Hall of Fame. We mentioned that it was about time Bruce and the Band played a live show in Liverpool. He agreed and said he would look into it!

Great seats in Newark
Kicking off with "Meet Me in the City," in Bruce's home state of New Jersey, the crowd was fantastic, especially during the songs where quiet is a must. You could hear a pin drop, and because of this,

"Point Blank," "Fade Away," "Drive All Night," and "Wreck on the Highway" became moments to cherish. Bruce dedicated the song "The River" to his sister Virginia and her husband Micky Shave, both in attendance that night, and danced with his mom during "Dancing In The Dark." At the end of the show, my wife and I looked at each other, smiled and walked out on a cloud while listening to Alison Krauss singing "Let's Go Down to the River and Pray," the air filled with the excitement of what we had just experienced and of what was to come.

In the pit at The Verizon Center, Washington DC, My Soul Sister! My Springsteen Buddy! My Lovely Wife, El

This trip was a great way to start the year. When the UK shows were announced, we decided on two shows because it's so physically demanding these days. We got GA for Manchester and Wembley; hoping to get in the pit!

A Rainy Manchester

Manchester was a tough day. We arrived at The Etihad at 7:30 am and were given numbers 178 and 179. Roll calls happened at the usual intervals, and we lined up starting at 12 o'clock, when the heavy rain started, and persisted until the show's end. Despite this, we were treated to a great set, with a trifecta of "Atlantic City," "Murder Incorporated," and "Badlands."

We got a pounding "Darkness on the Edge of Town," leading into a five-song River stretch, including a fantastic version of "I Wanna Marry You," "The River," and "Point Blank," and to open the encore, my favorite of the night, a mesmerizing "Backstreets." Bruce took us to the edge of the universe and beyond. This was the toughest show we had ever attended, physically and mentally, and by the end, we had absolutely nothing left in the tank. It was difficult to talk about the last three hours; we never felt like this coming out of a Springsteen show before. Our bodies seized up, and we found it difficult to walk back to the hotel. It was a long day, but we recovered by the next morning, and were able to reflect on the sheer joy of the experience.

Next, we went to Wembley Stadium. We travelled to Wembley the day before the show to join the roll call. We got numbers 229 and 230, once again a great spot in the pit. We met Jan and Graham Logan, who were lined up next to us on show day. They had also travelled 230 miles from Liverpool; a happy coincidence for us all. We had much to share, as they were both passionate and fanatical as we are about Bruce Springsteen, music, and life in general. We exchanged emails and have since met up back in Liverpool on numerous occasions.

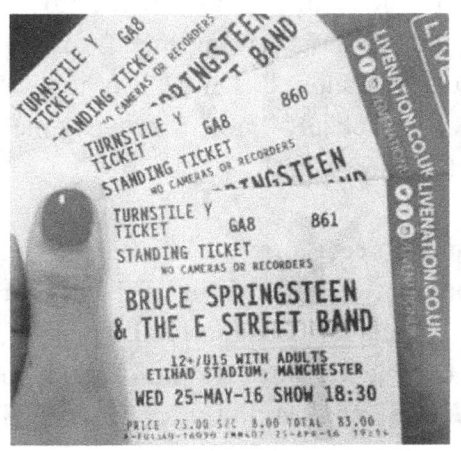

Pit at Wembley

We were treated to a solo piano version of "Does this Bus Stop at 82nd Street?" (Bruce needs to practice his whistling!) Next up was a blistering "Seeds," with Bruce strangling the neck off his guitar during the solo. We enjoyed the rarely played "Be True," followed by "Candy's Room" and "She's the One."

Bruce pulled a sign from the crowd: "I'll Work for Your Love." He decided to go solo acoustic but struggled to find the right key (much to the watching band's amusement), but once found he absolutely nailed it. Further into the set the mood changed during a serious and heartfelt "American Skin (41 Shots)".

The encore opened with a fan favourite, "Jungleland," then finishing with a solo acoustic of "Thunder Road." The end of another perfect day.

On our train journey back home, I had one of those moments where you start to lose all logical thought processes. (Best described as "about to enter Planet Springsteen") After arriving home, we decided to attend the show in Paris. Two hours later, we had flights, a hotel and two pit tickets – Paris, here we come! We were definitely back on Planet Springsteen.

Merci Beaucoup Pareee!

We got a great spot near the front of the pit, and there was electric anticipation in the air for Bruce to finally play "The River" in full for the first time ever in Europe. He didn't disappoint after the perfect opening of "The Iceman" and "Lucky Town." This was only the 4th time "The Iceman" had ever been performed live, and Bruce's guitar solo in "Lucky Town" was out of this world. We all knew what was coming next: *The River* from start to finish. It was the fourth time for us, and was just as enjoyable as all the others. It was a wonderful Parisian night.

We really thought this was our last show of the tour … until Jan and Graham told us that it was Graham's 60th birthday on August 28th, coinciding with the Chicago show. They "got a deal through Expedia and two great seats." During our return journey home, Eileen and I had another "Planet Springsteen moment." Coincidentally, the previous week, I received a few emails from the Rock and Roll Forever Foundation with information on pit tickets and great seats for the remaining American shows on the tour, so I emailed the Foundation, secured a few pit tickets, hotel room and flights; Chicago, here we come!

Hello Chicago

On this final American leg of the tour, Bruce had some surprises. He started with "New York City Serenade" and played songs from his first two albums, *Greetings from Asbury Park* and *The Wild, The Innocent,* throwing in "Jack of All Trades" with the strings, adding another dimension to the song.

For the Chicago show, he took quite a few signs from the crowd. We heard the rarely played "None But The Brave" and "New York City Serenade," and got a fantastic version of "Backstreets" to open the encore and he finished with a heartfelt "Bobby Jean," perhaps not a hardcore fan favourite, but for us, it was a question of; "Was this really our last show of the tour? Good Luck, Goodbye…"

On to Jersey

We usually take a late summer vacation to America around the last two weeks in September, which includes the date of our wedding anniversary, Sept. 23rd (also Springsteen's birthday). It's just a happy coincidence, I swear.

In August 2015, we booked a trip to New York City including a visit to the Museum at Bethel in the Woods, (the original site of the 1969 Woodstock festival) and a trip around New Jersey including a visit to Danny Federici's grave to pay our respects, Freehold, Asbury Park, and East Rutherford. Little did we know what would happen on this trip!

In June 2016, we found out that Bruce's autobiography, *Born to Run*, would be published on Sept. 27th, 2016. We had already booked our hotel at the Freehold Radisson that night. We wondered if Bruce would do a book signing in his hometown. Was it meant to be? Our friends were convinced it would happen; we could only hope!

Born to Run Book Launch

On Monday, Sept. 12th, I checked my iPad for any news. The night before, the Bruce Springsteen book tour had been leaked on the internet. The first event would be held at the Freehold Barnes and Noble on Sept. 27th. Could this really be happening? I phoned them and was told that tickets were available on the Eventbrite website. I logged in and got two tickets. We couldn't believe it. We were finally going to meet Bruce in person. All year, we had been saying, "Can it get any better than this?" And it did!

The day arrived. We parked, took our place in line, and Bruce turned up at 10:30. We were taken into the store, given a wristband, and paid for our books, which we would receive after meeting Bruce.

We finally got to meet Bruce at about 12:00 noon. We stepped onto the podium, shook his hand and told him we had travelled from Liverpool. He acknowledged this, and I said, "You've never played a live show in Liverpool; don't you think it's about time you did?" He responded, "Well, we'll have to see what we can do about that." The seed was sown! We got our photos, and then it was on to the next in line. A brief moment in time perhaps, but one we'll never forget. What a great way to give some of his most ardent fans a rare opportunity to spend a moment with him. I have never seen so many happy, smiling faces in one place. Later that afternoon, we went to the iconic Jersey Freeze for a scoop of peanut butter ice cream.

The Bruce Springsteen Collection, Monmouth University, 2016

Next, we moved on to Asbury Park. I arranged to visit the Bruce Springsteen Collection at Monmouth University with Eileen Chapman, the current custodian. We wanted to read the original *Time* and *Newsweek magazine* issues from 1975, with Bruce on the cover. Eileen had many stories to tell, and we had a great conversation about our hometown of Liverpool, The Beatles, The Cavern, The Stone Pony, Asbury Park and of course, Bruce.

Upon arriving back home in Liverpool, we reflected on our trip and where we were off to next. On Oct. 17th, Bruce appeared at Waterstones Piccadilly in London for another stop on his book tour, and on October 19th, he was interviewed on the BBC by Simon Mayo, who asked fans to submit a question via the BBC website. I wrote in and asked, "When are you going to play a show in Liverpool?" and it turned out that was the second most asked question. Bruce said, "We'll have to see." The idea was starting to gain momentum, so I contacted the Liverpool Echo with my Freehold story to see if we could push this forward. They phoned me back for an interview, and the rest is history. (Story link)

It was an amazing first year in retirement. Remember … it all starts with the music, without which we have nothing.

Phil's blog: Lifelong Bruce Springsteen Fan
http://www.thelightindarkness.com/news/phil-beard-lifelong-bruce-springsteen-fan/

Lenny from NJ

In 1981, I went to the Stone Pony with a girl that I was dating on and off to see a band called Cats on a Smooth Surface, with hopes that Bruce might show up, as he had many times before. We stood in line for hours to ensure we got close to the stage and finally got in to see the band. Late in the evening, Bruce indeed showed up, to the delight of fans, and played a few songs.

When the set was over, at the end of the night, we strategically positioned ourselves near the door, hoping to get a glimpse of Bruce. As he left the building, Lori, the girl I was with (and the author of this book), asked Bruce, "Can I get a picture with you?" He replied, "Sure!" She handed me the camera, and I was able to snap this now-famous picture of Bruce and Lori that is on the cover of her website. Unfortunately, I was on the other side of the camera, and since selfies didn't exist yet, and the camera flash took forever to recharge, I didn't get a picture with Bruce. But it was a great encounter that I will never forget.

Bob Fuller, Staten Island NY

In 1983, my future wife and I were on the same train heading home from work in Manhattan. The music she was listening to caught my ear, and she caught my eye. Her beauty and choice of music really hooked me: the sax solo from "Rosalita!" *Wow, I MUST talk to her.* Soon, we started dating. Forty one years and 23 shows later, we are still married and will be forever grateful for "Rosalita" because it was through that song that I met the love of my life.

The greatest show I ever saw was on April 22, 2016, in Newark, NJ, the night after Prince passed away. The stage went dark and then turned purple! Bruce played "Purple Rain." There was not a dry eye in the house.

Another special memory was in Sept. of 2003 at the old Giants Stadium. We took my older brother and sister, who have since both passed away. Bruce brought in sand, a lifeguard stand, a carousel and a ferris wheel. It was hysterical. My brother and sister had the time of their lives; it was the first and only time they saw him.

Jimmy Baron, Atlanta, GA

One evening in 2007, I got a call from a friend who worked for Columbia Records. He told me that Bruce was in Atlanta quietly working on a project with record producer Brendan O'Brien (it turned out to be the *Magic* album) and was staying at the Four Seasons hotel. I knew from legendary stories that Bruce would sometimes hang out at various hotel bars with fans, so I figured it was worth a shot.

I grabbed a friend and went down to the Four Seasons bar, which was completely empty. We sat at a table and after about half an hour, to our surprise, Bruce meandered up to the entrance of the bar, solo, and peeked in to see if there was anything going on - which there wasn't. I mustered up the courage to approach him and threw out a "Hi Bruce. How are you liking Atlanta? Been to a Braves game yet?" (he had), and he politely engaged in small talk.

And then, out of nowhere, I blurted out, "Hey, can I buy you a beer?" to which he shockingly answered, "Sure!"

So he and I made our way to a separate table and had a beer, uninterrupted, for half an hour! We were still the only ones there, other than a small group of drunk conventioneers hanging in the corner. I remember that we chatted about parenthood (I was about to become a first-time dad) and various cities he liked or didn't like, but truthfully, I couldn't hear much of what he was saying because of the loud voice inside my head that kept screaming over and over "HOLY SHIT, I'M HAVING A BEER WITH BRUCE SPRINGSTEEN!!!"

He obliged me with a picture, thanked me, and left.

When I got home, I could barely speak. My heart was racing. I woke up my wife and told her, through hyperventilating, "Honey, you'll never guess what just happened!!!" To which she responded deadpan from a deep sleep, "You met Springsteen." I answered, "YES, how did you know?" She replied, "Because that's the only thing that could make you this excited."

Tribute to Brady

There are moments in life when music transcends into something beyond words. Reaching beyond its role as mere entertainment, the music becomes something more—something deeply personal and profoundly moving.

For me, that moment came on April 11, 2023, at the UBS Arena in Long Island, during a Bruce Springsteen concert.

Brady, our beloved, forever 15-year-old son and guardian angel, who was incredibly loving, caring, funny, and smart, had a deep love for Springsteen's music. We shared countless memories centered around Bruce songs, and these moments brought us closer. On April 11, 2023, I was supposed to be in the pit with Brady. Unfortunately, Brady had other plans and was in his seat in heaven. I wanted Bruce to know Brady, to feel his spirit, and to understand how much his music meant to my son, so I made a sign.

I wasn't hoping for much—just a simple acknowledgment, something small. As Bruce played "Promised Land," one of Brady's favorite songs, I held up the sign. At that moment, Bruce walked by, looked me directly in the eyes, and blew me a kiss. My friend Jay, along with my Springnuts friends Laurie and Joe, were in awe. They turned to me and said, "He's going to do something special."

The anticipation grew, but I couldn't have imagined what happened next. During "10th AvenueFreeze-Out," Bruce came over to where I was standing. I thought he wanted to shake my hand, but instead, he gestured for me to give him the sign. I handed it to him, and at that moment, Bruce took the sign on stage and dedicated "I'll See You in My Dreams" to Brady. After the song ended, he said, "RIP Brady," and returned the sign to me.

It was an experience that words cannot express. At that moment, Bruce Springsteen not only acknowledged Brady's memory but honored it in a way that I will never forget. Brady was there with us and will continue to live on in our hearts and dreams.

Thank you, Bruce, for your music, for bringing me closer to my son, and for your kindness in honoring those that have passed. Brady, we are grateful and thankful for the wonderful 15 years you shared with us. We love you deeply and always! We miss you.

I'll See You in My Dreams, Brady.

Afterward

Thank you to those who submitted their stories. And thank you, Bruce, for being a beacon of hope, connection, and joy. We are grateful.

www.ingramcontent.com/pod-product-compliance
Lightning Source LLC
Chambersburg PA
CBHW071914070526
44583CB00016B/1985